Elegie

Alto Saxophone

arat

Edited by H. Voxman

Allegretto Brillante

Alto Saxophone

J. Demersseman
Arranged by H. Voxman

Alto Saxophone

Andante And Allegro

Alto Saxophone

Andre Chailleux
Edited by H. Voxman

Alto Saxophone

Badine

Scherzo

Alto Saxophone

Gabriel - Marie
Arranged by Henry W. Davis

Alto Saxophone

Canzonetta

Alto Saxophone

A. d'Ambrosio
Arranged by Herman A. Hummel

Alto Saxophone

Carnival Of Venice
Air Varie

Alto Saxophone

Henry W. Davis

Alto Saxophone

Polovtsian Dance

Alto Saxophone

From "Prince Igor"

Alexander Borodin
Arranged by Harold L. Walters

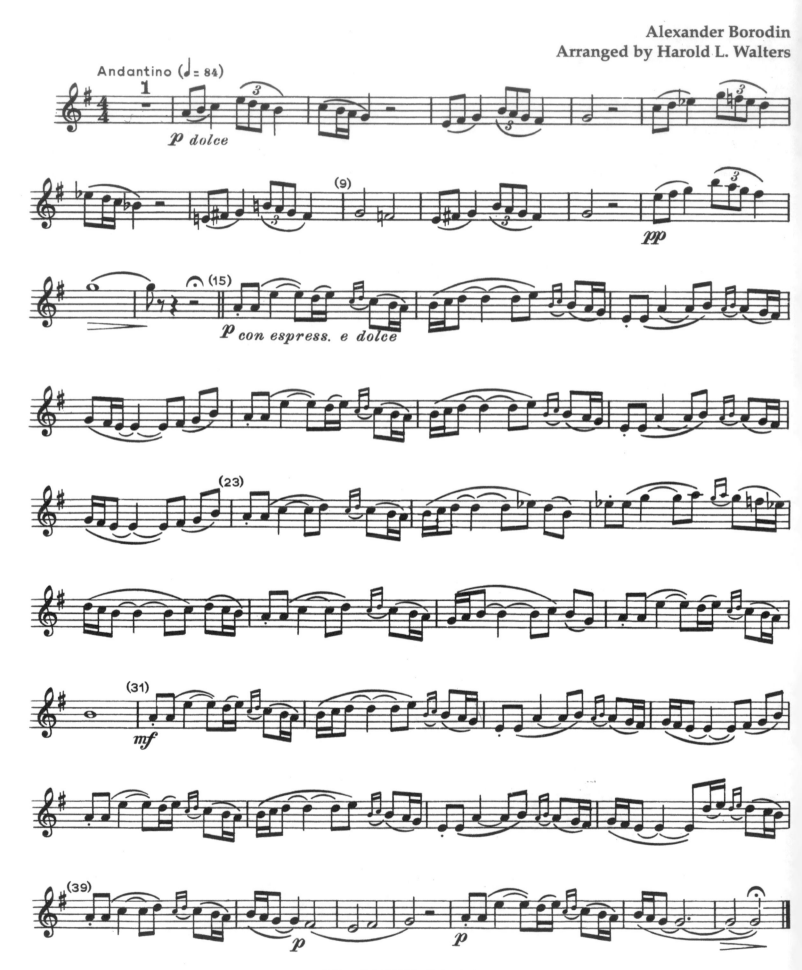

Solo de L'Arlesienne
Based on the Music to "L'Arlesienne"

Alto Saxophone

George Bizet
Arranged by Herman A. Hummel

Time of performance : 5:30.

For shorter performance (4:00) eliminate repeats in the Minuetto, and cut from ⊕ to ⊕

Alto Saxophone

Alto Saxophone

Le Carillon
Allegretto moderato (♩ = 120)

Estilian Caprice

Alto Saxophone

Gene Paul

Alto Saxophone

The Duchess

Alto Saxophone

Richard H. Rehl

Alto Saxophone

Alto Saxophone

Alto Saxophone

*) NOTE: In 4th & 5th measures use low D♭ & C fingering with octave key.

Hungarian Dance No. 5

Alto Saxophone

Johannes Brahms
Arranged by Henry W. Davis